DELPHI

DELPHI

Text by
GEORGIA TARSOULI

PUBLISHERS
M. PECHLIVANIDES & Co

●

CENTRAL DISTRIBUTORS
«ATLANTIS» S.A.
KORAI 8 ● ATHENS

Every famous site of Ancient Greece has its particular character and beauty. On the Acropolis of Athens all is light and harmony. Olympia is an achievement in perfect proportion, in surroundings of serene tranquillity. Most legendary of all is Delphi. The wild beauty of its natural setting and its austere grandeur fill every visitor with awe.

On the southern slopes of Parnassos a narrow mountainous vale separates the main massif from the adjoining range of Kirphis. Delphi lies in an amphitheatre at a height of 1900 feet above the steep ravines of the valley. Behind tower two enormous rocks, soaring to a height of another 1000 feet and divided by a steep gorge. They are the famous Phaedriades, which form an unapproachable barrier to the north. Closed in on all other sides by gigantic rocks and mountain ranges, the western horizon opens out into the most wonderful panorama in the world. For at the foot of Delphi stretches the fertile plain of Amphissa, with its thousand–year old olive grove gleaming like a silvery–green sea, while the real waters of the Corinthian Gulf vanish beyond it in the distance like a mirror.

In the middle of this wonderful landscape the Ancient Greeks placed their most important sanctuary, the Oracle of Pythian Apollo. Of that sanctuary and the splendid buildings that surrounded it only ruins remain today. But those ruins and their astonishing frame–work are sufficient to stir the visitor deeply and to make the ancient glory of Delphi live again.

*F*or nearly a thousand years, from the seventh century B.C. till the fourth century A.D., Delphi was the greatest religious and cultural centre of the known world. It swayed the destinies of men and nations and had a powerful influence on the development of religion and education, literature and art, colonisation and trade.

The oracle itself has a remote and ancient past. Early traditions tell how it stood at the entrance to a steaming chasm and was guarded by a terrible serpent called the Python. The oracle was dedicated to Gaia, the primitive Earth Goddess. But as Delphi was often convulsed by earthquakes it was also sacred to Poseidon, the Sea God and Earth–Shaker. Time went by and the oracle became the centre of a new worship – that of Apollo. Some say that the God arrived in Greece on a dolphin from Crete and call him Delphinios Apollo. Others know him as Hyperborean Apollo and say that he came from the far north. But all agree that the young Apollo, the God of Light, slew the venomous serpent and took possession of the oracle. Through its voice he revealed the will of his father Zeus and guided men towards a higher civilization.

The early oracles were delivered in the cave of the Python and the virgin priestess continued to be known as the Pythia. Seated on a sacred tripod and shrouded in the veils of her office, she chewed on laurel leaves until she fell into a frenzied trance. As she uttered her prophecies they were recorded by the priest and set in oracular verse for the pilgrims.

At first the oracle was only a centre of pilgrimage for men of nearby states, who consulted it on local or family matters. Gradually its reputation spread. Kings, rulers and famous personalities asked for advice on the most serious problems of the day. The oracle's answers were usually solutions of common sense. Its priesthood was wise with the insight of long years of experience. Unable to prevent the wars that rent the Greek states, the oracle was a successful mediator and imposed the first rules of international law. Rival states were forbidden to destroy each other's acqueducts or to pollute wells. They also bound themselves not to slaughter their prisoners.

When the Greeks formed their first association of states, Delphi was chosen as its centre. The alliance was known as the Amphiktyonic League. Its founder members were twelve neighbouring tribes, living between Mount Olympus and the Gulf of Corinth. They took a solemn oath to respect each other's cities — «No Amphiktyon shall molest the other.» Later, the League increased its importance and allied the Thessalian tribes to the Ionians and Dorians. Twice a year, in spring and autumn, representatives of all the member states met and discussed current problems. They sat in judgement when cities accused their neighbours of aggression and were empowered to impose sanctions or even to declare war on the offender.

On one occasion, in 596 B.C., one of these «holy» wars was declared on behalf of Delphi itself. The Amphiktyonic League authorised Solon of Athens and Cleisthenes of Sikyon to punish the people of Crissa, the inhabitants of the modern plain of Amphissa, for exploiting pilgrims to the sanctuary and forcing them to pay exhorbitant taxes. Crissa was destroyed and its fertile plain was dedicated to Apollo. The League then decided to hold a solemn festival at Delphi every four years. All the Greek states took part, but Athens had the place of honour in recognition of her leading services in this war. A general truce was proclaimed at the time of the festival, which consisted of religious ceremonies, a pageant representing the slaying of the Python and a number of artistic and athletic contests. The last were a later addition to the celebrations. A hippodrome for chariot races was built on the plain of Crissa and a stadium was carved in the mountain-side, high above the temple.

The great temple of Apollo was the centre of the Delphic cult. The first primitive shrine is said to have been a simple hut of wattled branches, cut from the laurel, the tree of Daphne. The legend of Daphne tells how Apollo loved this chaste nymph, who was changed by Mother Earth into a laurel bush to save her from his embraces. Ever afterwards the laurel was sacred to the disconsolate God.

Later, a stone temple was built on the site of the shrine. In 548 B.C. it was destroyed by fire. Three thousand talents, (equivalent to some $ 750,000), were needed to build a temple worthy of the oracle's growing reputation. A call went out for contributions and all the Greek cities of Asia Minor, mainland Greece and Italy sent their share. Handsome donations were made by the wealthy Croesus, King of Lydia, and Amassis, Pharaoh of Egypt. The largest contribution of all was made by a noble family of Athens, the Alcmeonides, who completed the amount necessary to rebuild the temple and decorate it with marble.

The great prestige and wealth of Delphi date from that time. Gifts of priceless value were sent from near and far, the sanctuary was embellished by votive offerings, statues and temple-like buildings known as «Treasuries», where the cities kept their gifts to Apollo.

When the Persians attacked Greece, a Persian force detached from the main army arrived at Delphi to plunder the temple. But, as Herodotus mentions: «*Thunderbolts fell on them from the sky and two pinnacles of rock, torn from Parnassus, came crashing and rumbling down amongst them, while at the same time there was a great cry from inside the shrine.*» All Greece knew that Apollo had intervened to save his sanctuary.

At the end of the war the grateful victors honoured the God who had prophesied that their «wooden walls» would save them. New votive offerings, trophies won from their enemies at Marathon and Salamis, statues and tripods bearing the names of the cities which had resisted the barbarians were erected near the temple. New treasuries were built and filled with precious offerings.

It was only natural that all this accumulating wealth should arouse the neighbours' rapacity. Delphi went through three more holy wars. The last two gave Philip of Macedon the excuse to descend upon Greece from Macedonia, at the call of the Amphiktyons. His victory of Chaeronia was destined to change the course of Greek history.

*T*wo hundred and ten years after the Persian attack, in 279 B.C., another barbarian race invaded Greece - the Galatians. This time, Apollo allowed them to penetrate to the very gates of the sanctuary. Then he slung stones and rocks from the Phaedriades and forced them to retreat, pursued by the people of Aetolia and Phocis, saving Delphi a second time from the pillage of the barbarians. But he was unable to avert the final decline and devastation. The fame of Delphi was gradually diminishing. Alexander the Great had violated the holy of holies and forced the Pythia to give the oracle he wished. Sulla had plundered the temples of their votive offerings to meet the expenses of the siege of Athens. It is true that Augustus and Hadrian supported the sanctuary and Herod Atticus rebuilt the Stadium. But Nero took away five hundred of the statues and the soldiers of Constantine the Great carried off the most beautiful works of art to Constantinople to decorate the new capital. Finally, Theodosius closed the oracle and forbade the ancient worship. It is said that the pagan and utopian Emperor Julian the Apostate, who tried to reinstate the Greek religion, sent to consult the oracle of Delphi and that the Pythia, more clearsighted than he, made the famous reply.

«*Tell ye the King, the carven hall is fallen in decay;*
Apollo hath no chapel left, no prophesying bay,
No talking spring. The stream is dry that had so much to say».

Whether the story is true or not, the oracle never spoke again. Goths and Slavs destroyed what was left of Delphi and earthquakes completed its ruin, covering its remains with earth. The hamlet of Kastri stood on the site of the famous sanctuary when Greek and foreign archaeologists began to investigate the area of Delphi in the past century, and located the site. France had the honour of revealing ancient Delphi to the world. A grant of 750,000 gold francs was voted by the French Government for the purpose, and the Greek Government subscribed 60,000 drachmas to rebuild the village further to the west. Systematic excavations began in 1891 and continued until 1903. The temple, the theatre, the stadium, the treasuries, all the buildings of Delphi, returned to the light of day, and with them 6,000 inscriptions and some of the greatest ancient works of art. We see them today in the Museum and try to conjure up an image of the splendour of this most famous of ancient sanctuaries.

Delphi is 100 miles from Athens through Arachova and 150 miles if you take the picturesque Gravia road, passing through Amphissa, with its historic medieval castle. Another road approaches Delphi from Patras, across Rion ferry. But the route for leisurely travellers is via Itea, the harbour of Delphi. They can enjoy all the gleaming beauty of the Gulf of Corinth and the fascination of the age old olive groves of Amphissa, stretching for nearly 10 miles to the foot of Mount Parnassos. Whichever way you come, the first sight of Delphi is stupendous. The breathtaking heights of the Phaedriades hide even Parnassos - twin pinnacles set by the God to protect his sanctuary. Some titanic hand has sundered them in two and formed a narrow ravine, whence spring the sacred waters of Castalia. The ancient name «Phaedriades» means «gleaming» and their modern names have been earned for the same reason. One rock is called «Rodini» on account of its rosy colour and the other is known as «Phlemboukos» because it reddens in the sunset.

Below the rocks and across the modern road are the ruins of the sanctuary of Athena Pronaia, shining white amid the wild flowers and shaded by silver olives, with the slender columns of the Tholos. We follow in the steps of the ancient pilgrims and of Pausanias. Although the latter found the Tholos erect and undamaged, he did not explain the use of this attractive round building. Three of its twenty columns have been re-erected, with a portion of the epistyle and the frieze, giving us some idea of its ancient beauty. Unfortunately, both the more recent temple of Athena Pronaia and the older one, destroyed in ancient days by the fall of a rock, are completely ruined and we leave them for the Gymnasium and the Palestra, or wrestling ground, where we see the round bathing pool for the young athletes. On the high supporting wall are the openings of the water cocks. Now they are dry, but in olden days they brought unlimited water from the Castalian spring.

Returning to the road, we see the spring itself. Its waters may be less abundant than they used to be, but they are as cool as ever and crystal clear. Modern beauty lovers — we wash our hands and wet our hair as did the ancient pilgrims, and go beneath the pine trees to find the Sacred Way.

If you look at a plan of the sanctuary of Delphi, many famous names appear along the Sacred Way – the «Marathon Votive Offering», the «Argive Kings», the «Treasury of the Sikyonians». But of all these only the bases remain, with an inscription that marks the site, as the winding pavestones mount the slope. Turning a corner, we come upon an attractive marble structure, the Treasury of the Athenians, built as a thank offering to Apollo a few years after the victory of Marathon. In 1904 the Municipality of Athens, very appropriately, gave the money for its restoration. A little higher up are the elegant Ionic columns of the Stoa of the Athenians, which sheltered the trophies won at Salamis, the greatest naval battle of all time. Before reaching the Stoa, some rough hewn dusty stones are conspicuous amid the marble fragments. They mark the site of the most awesome precincts in Delphi, the sanctuary of Gaia the Earth, where Apollo slew the Python and where the first Pythia uttered her prophecies. Time, and his own hands, have destroyed the works of man, but Mother Earth has preserved her sanctuary inviolate through centuries and aeons.

A lofty, strong-built polygonal wall is the first gigantic stairway to the Temple of Apollo. It was built to support the slope and to surround the temple precincts. This wall is covered from top to bottom with over 800 inscriptions, recording decisions of the Amphiktyons, releases of slaves, athletic victories, etc. It is a valuable source of information and perhaps the most ancient journal in the world.

One more turn brings us to the entrance of the temple. A notice to our right marks the site of the «Plataea Votive Offering». Here stood the bronze triple serpent with the names of 31 cities who had fought the Persians at Plataea. The golden tripod held in place by the serpents' heads was stolen by the Phocians in the second holy war. Constantine the Great carried off the remains to Constantinople, where they can still be seen today in the Hippodrome, headless and half-buried. All that is left in Delphi is the round base on which it stood.

The temple opposite us is not that built by the Alcmeonides. That temple was destroyed by earthquakes in 372 B.C., and was rebuilt by all-Greek subscription. Colonists in far off Crimea, Sicily and Africa sent their share. Nothing is left, even of the second temple.

The walls have been levelled to the ground and only four or five of its 42 Doric columns were in a fit state for restoration. Even these are mutilated and broken. It is difficult to trace the layout of the temple and to identify the shrine, the sanctuary of the Pythia and the hall for the waiting pilgrims.

Grief at so great a destruction is forgotten when we climb the steep flight of steps leading to the Theatre. There is nothing to betray its presence in advance. Suddenly we find ourselves in its calyx-shaped precincts, scooped out of the heart of the rock. Wonderful mountain scenery forms its background.

In 1927, the inspired initiative of the poet Angelos Sikelianos and his American born wife Eva caused the thundering voice of «Prometheus Bound» invoking divine justice to be heard again after two thousand years, whilst eagles, the sacred birds of Zeus, circled around the Phaedriades above his head. The audience, many of them intellectuals and critics from all parts of Europe and America, listened spellbound. It was the first time that the re-discovered theatre came back to life. Today both Angelos and Eva Sikelianos are buried in a humble tomb, 500 metres from the theatre. But their memory lives on. These first Delphic Festivals had a fundamental influence on the modern interpretation of ancient drama.

To the west of the theatre, a path leads up to the Stadium. This is not the ancient Stadium where Pindar watched the Pythian Games. It was built in 180 A.D. by a rich Athenian, Herod Atticus, who also donated an all-marble stadium to Athens.

To the generosity of a modern patriot and benefactor, Andreas Syngros, we owe the Museum of Delphi. It stands on the highway, between the Phaedriades and the village, and contains all the works of sculpture found on the site, fragments of buildings, metopes and reliefs, statues, votive offerings and other works of art. At the entrance we admire the famous «Navel of the Earth» - a relic of the ancient fetish worship. In the first room on the right is a reconstruction of the «Treasury of the Siphnians», with its wonderful archaic Caryatids, elder sisters of the Caryatids of the Erechtheion, yet more sophisticated, with their flimsy Ionian tunics fastened on the shoulder, their little ears pierced for ear-rings and dark tresses curled in the complicated and elaborate hair style of the sixth century. The pediment represents the quarrel between Apollo and Hercules, who struggles to seize the Delphic tripod. The frieze shows the Gods of Olympus, on one side as interested spectators of a battle between Greeks and Trojans and on the other as active participants in the battle against the Giants.

The severe and enigmatic Sphynx of the Naxians stands nearby. Its lion's feet were once supported by an Ionic column, ten metres high, slightly below the Stoa of the Athenians.

The pillar supporting the three graceful dancers of the Acanthus rose like the stem of a flower, 28 feet high. Their feet rest on the dark bristly leaves which form the capital of the pillar. The folds of their short tunic catch on their knees. They hold it up with one hand, while the other supports their round headgear. Many say that they are «Thyades», but their virgin grace, modest expression and sweet faces ill accord with the wild transports of the followers of Bacchus.

The Museum contains many other statues, reliefs and inscriptions. Some of them attract at first sight. Others require longer for their charm to be fully appreciated. Some need an expert to explain them. Only two or three of the metopes from the Treasury of the Athenians, representing the feats of Hercules and Theseus, are preserved more or less intact. Fragments of the friezes of the great temple remain, belonging to the Temple of the Alcmeonides and buried by the ancient Greeks themselves. They contain the hymn to Apollo imbedded in the walls of the Treasury of the Athenians. The words of the hymn are fine, but the most important discovery are the small marks under each syllable, the musical score and the only surviving example of ancient notation.

Other exhibits not to be missed are the statues of Cleon and Biton, donated by the Argives in commemoration of the two devoted sons of the priestess of Hera, the statue of Agias, the handsome all in wrestler, which for years was believed to be the work of Lysippus, and the melancholy Antinous, favorite of Hadrian, whose mournful beauty decorates nearly every museum. There is the charming head of a little girl, standing on a body which does not belong to it, and a fine marble head of a philosopher. But the last room draws us like a magnet. There, alone on a low pedestal, is Delphi's most valuable possession, the bronze Charioteer. Few ancient bronze statues have survived to this day. While marble figures were pulled down or broken, bronze was put to more practical uses. It was forged into a suit of armour, or a household copper. Later it was used to make canons. The sea was more kind to the bronze gods and heroes sunk in its depths in the Roman galleys that foundered off the Greek headlands. It is to the sea that we owe the ephebes of Antikythera and Marathon, the little jockey and the Zeus of Artemisium. But the Charioteer was preserved by the soil of Delphi. In the earthquake of 372 B.C. he fell from his pedestal, where he stood driving his chariot above the north end of the temple. He was covered so deep in earth and stones that no-one attempted to dig him out. The temple was rebuilt and other statues filled his place. Romans, Byzantines, Franks, and Turks came there in turn. The ruin of Delphi was complete. But the Charioteer lay unharmed in his grave awaiting the day when he should see the light once more.

Now he stands before us, tall, upright, with his long tunic falling in straight folds, the right hand raised to hold the reins. He is still only a youth! The first down has barely appeared on his cheek and he is as slim as a cypress. In other statues we appreciate the play of the muscles, the modelling and movement of the body. The Charioteer has nothing of this. It is the expression concentrated in his eyes and the half-open youthful mouth, that we admire. He is a victor, still giddy from the contest, the triumph and the cheers, and he has not yet left his chariot. The face expresses the modest pride of a young hero, who does not let himself be dazzled by a fleeting victory. He gazes into the distance. Only his slightly opened lips betray fatigue and slight vertigo. The hand holding the reins is steady, the feet are planted firmly side by side. These two naked feet have been moulded with loving care and deserve a treatise in themselves. The artist knew that nobody would see them, that they would be hidden behind the chariot at a height where no human eye could reach. It was for his own pleasure and satisfaction that he made them flawless.

After leaving the Museum we need a resting-place to think over our impressions. The road leads into the village. Wherever you sit, in coffee house or modern tourist hotel, your eyes travel from the steep slopes of Parnassos to the green olive groves and the smooth surface of the Gulf of Corinth. Relaxed and refreshed, you breathe in the beauty of the landscape.

When the time comes to leave, there are pleasures on the way back. Do not hurry to return to the noise and bustle of town!

On the way to Levadia you will pass through the village of Arachova, perched like the eyrie of an eagle on the slopes of Parnassos. Its tall bell tower can be seen from afar, on the top of a crag that juts above the ravine like a lofty balcony. High above the village rises the church of St. George, patron saint and sentinel. Close to this spot, late in November 1826, during the War of Independence, the Greek general Karaiskakis won the famous battle of Arachova. The fight lasted three days. The Greek general's gun emplacements can still be seen in the church. St. George himself is said to have come on his white horse and helped the Greeks to win. Any old inhabitant of Arachova, asked about the miracle, will tell you that his grandfather saw the Saint with his own eyes charging his foes sword in hand. As Delphi founded the festival of the «Sotiria» to honour Apollo for saving them from the Galatians of Brennus, so Arachova honours St. George. Old and young come from all the neighbouring villages on St. George's Day, April 23rd. The women wear their embroidered kerchiefs, their red aprons and heavy necklaces. The men of Arachova are in fustanellas. The celebrations last for three days, as did the battle. Masses are held in honour of the Saint and old and young surpass themselves in curling contests, wrestling bouts and jumping competitions. As evening falls, dancing and singing start – to continue beyond the dawn.

If you chance to arrive at this time, the Pythian tradition will seem to come alive. But even on an ordinary day Arachova should not be missed, with its delicious phromaella cheese, its kneaded bread and famous red wine. All-wool rugs are woven by the women on their looms, in severe patterns and colours handed down by their great-grandmothers. And if a rug or a sheepskin mat is too much to carry, there are attractive embroidered shopping bags to take as souvenirs of Arachova.

Twelve miles further on, three roads meet in a narrow pass. The ancient Greeks called it the «Schisti Odos» and now it is known as the «Crossroads of Megas». Here Oedipus met his father Laius. He killed him, not knowing who he was, because he would not let him pass, and started the series of calamities which beset the House of Thebes. And on a summer afternoon in 1856 a young officer called Ioannis Megas with his small troop surprised the bandit chief Davelis and his men and wiped them out. Megas fell, fighting gallantly, and his effigy has been carved on a neighbouring rock, with a few words to commemorate his courageous exploit.

Here is the turn to Distomo and the monastery of Osios Loukas. But modern travellers would do better to take the earlier turning, three miles back towards Arachova.

This monastery is known as a Royal foundation, for legend has it that the church was built by the Emperor Romanus II, father of Basil II. But the real founder was Osios Loukas, Holy Luke the Steiriote, a hermit born at the end of the ninth century. With others who had renounced the world, he built a hermitage over the ruined temple of Artemis Steiriotissa. There he spent his life in prayer, fasting and good works. He became so saintly that when he prayed his feet seemed to leave the ground. The fame of his miracles spread throughout Greece. When Crete was liberated from the Saracens, the Emperor Romanus wished to show his gratitude to the holy hermit, who had died in 946 A.D. «He called for experienced builders and gave them their orders, sending them to build a most beautiful church over the Saint's tomb. So excellent, marvellous, imposing and regal is the church of this monastery, so great its majesty, the multitude of its porphyry pillars, its wonderful marble panelling, its mosaic art and precious stones, that a similar church is not to be found today in Mount Athos, nor in any other place in Greece.»

That is how the old chronicler describes the monastery of Osios Loukas. Doubtless, his account is a mixture of imagination and truth. We do not know who was the real builder of the monastery, but we know that the church and its mosaics date from the eleventh century. And it is true that, with Daphni, Osios Loukas is the most beautiful, and least damaged Byzantine church left today, and that there is not a church like it «in Mount Athos, or in any other place in Greece.»

Monasteries were fortified strongholds in ancient times. This Boeotian monastery was fortified from Byzantine days until the years of the Greek War of Independence. Hence the strong surrounding wall and the high tower that surmounts the double-barred courtyard gate. Within are the cells of the monks – most of them empty today, and on the left is an ancient well, with running water and a drinking cup. The church stands on the right. In actual fact, there are three churches. Underneath is the crypt, with the tomb of Osios Loukas and four other tombs, whose occupants are unknown. This underground church was built as a foundation for the large upper Church, and is known as St. Barbara's. Next to the main church is the church of Our Lady, whose lovely frescoes have been destroyed by time and the hand of man. Its only ornaments now are its pillars and wonderful mosaic floor. Last and finest is the main church. As its hymnist says: «All this divine church glitters.» And it does really glitter. The floor is elaborately paved. The walls are covered half way up with many - coloured marble panels. From there to the top of the apses and domes, it is decorated with coloured mosaics on a gold ground.

One should s it for hours enjoying the mosaics of Osios Loukas one by one, and studying the scenes and personalities they portray. Hurried visitors cast a fleeting look around and then look at the reredos, preserved intact from ancient times. There they kneel before the ikons of Damascinos, the master of El Greco, with their carved marble frames. Whoever has more time to spare should see the outside of the church, with its elegant design, the ornamental bands of brick around its walls, and the beautifully wrought pillars of the dome of Our Lady's church.

At the end of the day, we sit and rest in the big square outside the monastery, shaded by an enormous plane tree. The slopes of Helicon are lost in blue and pink mist. Below are the slender branches of the almond trees. Sheepbells tinkle and evening falls slowly. A friendly inn is ready with food and shelter. Our rapid journey has taken us across the ancient, medieval and modern history of Greece. Before contemporary life resumes its hold, let us spend our few remaining hours enjoying the beauties of ageless Nature.

GEORGIA TARSOULI

2　The road to Delphi runs through groves of venerable olive trees, with silvery foliage,　3
and the green of tufted pine woods.

*

*C'est a travers des oliviers millénaires au feuillage d'argent et des pins touffus que passe
la route qui conduit a Delphes.*

*

*Zwischen tausendjæhrigen Olivenbæumen und gruenen, buschigen Kiefern fuehrt
der Weg nach Delphi.*

4

Phot.: V. & N. Tombasis

Our first stop is Levadia, now the capital of Boeotia. Its medieval bridge spans a river with an ancient name, the Erkyna, and the path along its bank leads to the fountain of Mnemosyne and the oracle of Trophonius.

*

Livadia, en Béotie, est notre première étape. Son pont moyenageux franchit une rivière au nom antique, l'Erkyna, et le sentier, sur le flanc de la montagne, conduit à la source de Mnémosyne et à l'oracle de Trophonios.

*

Die erste Station auf dem Wege nach Delphi ist Lewadia, die beruehmte Hauptstadt Bœotiens. Die mittelalterliche Bruecke fuehrt ueber den Herkyna-Fluss.

Phot. : A. Economides

Off the main road and beyond Distomo we come to the monastery of Hosios Loukas. Built in a picturesque valley on the slopes of Mt. Helicon, it is one of the most beautiful in Greece.

*

Le monastère d'Hosios Loucas, construit dans une vallée pittoresque, presque au flanc de l'Hélicon, est un des plus beaux monastères byzantins de Grèce.

*

Abseits von der Strasse finden wir in einem malerischen Tal das Kloster Hosios Lukas.

7

Two churches side by side, Holy Luke and Our Lady. Features of their architecture are the two dissimilar domes: The one large, round and low, the other high and delicately wrought, with graceful marble pillasters.

*

Ses églises, la principale et celle de la Vierge, construites tout près l'une de l'autre, présentent, malgré les traits communs de leur architecture, deux coupoles tout à fait différentes.

*

Das Kloster hat zwei Kirchen. Die eine ist dem Heilig. Lukas geweiht, die andere der Mutter Gottes. Sie sind beide im gleichen Stil erbaut, unterscheiden sich aber in der Form der Kuppel.

Phot. : V. & N. Tombasis

9   Phot.: V. & N. Tombasis

Outside the monastery, pilgrims
and travellers take their rest, in
the shade of an ancient plane tree.
While the old monk, who has renounced the world, passes by im-
passive, bucket in hand.

*

Sur l'esplanade qui s'étend devant
le monastère, sur la «Place des
Canons», a l'ombre d'un platane
géant, le voyageur peut prendre
un peu de repos et se rafraîchir,
tandis qu'un vieux moine qui
a renoncé aux vanités de ce monde
passe indifférent, son seau a la
main.

*

Von der grossen Platane am «Platz
der Kanonen» hat man eine be-
sonders schœne Aussicht, waehrend
ein Blick in den Klosterhof Erin-
nerungen an lœngst vergangene
Jahrhunderte wachruft.

10

«*This divine church shines throughout, surpassing any church in the world*», says the old hymnist. On the dome of the sanctuary is the wonderful mosaic of Pentecost, showing the twelve apostles with tongues of fire above their heads. In the recess below is the Virgin, with the holy child on her knee. Above a doorway one of the most beautiful mosaics shows the Virgin, holding the Child on her right arm.

*

«*Cette église divine resplendissante surpasse toutes les autres églises du monde*». C'est ainsi qu'une vielle hymne décrit l'église d'Hosios Loucas. Dans la coupole au-dessus du sanctuaire, l'admirable mosaïque, de la Pentecôte nous montre les douze apôtres avec les langues de feu au-dessus de leurs têtes, et dans l'abside nous voyons la Vierge tenan l'enfant divin sur ses genoux tandis qu'une autre mosaïque la presente le tenant sur son bras droit.

*

«*Dieser heilige Tempel ueberstrahlt alle Tempel der Welt* sagt die alte Hymne. Ein beruehmtes Mosaik zeigt di zwœlf Apostel. Eines der vier Mosaiken unter der Kuppel stellt die Muttergottes dar Neben der Pforte ist ebenfalt eins zu bewundern.

Phot.: V. & N. Tombasis

No other Byzantine church sparkles like Hosios Loukas with the gold of its mosaics. Even the patterns around the Apostles and archangels are framed in gold.

*

Aucune autre église byzantine ne resplendit autant de l'or de ses mosaïques que celle d'Hosios Loucas. Les figures des apôtres et des archanges, se détachent sur un fond d'or.

*

Kein anderes byzantinisches Kloster hat soviel Goldglanz in seinen Mosaiken wie Hosios Lukas.

An austere figure in a doorway recess is St. Basil, one of the three fathers of the Orthodox church.

*

Saint Basile, un des trois grands prélats de l'orthodoxie, réputés pour leur profonde sagesse.

*

Das Bild des heiligen Basilius strahlt schœne Strenge aus.

Phot.: V. & N. Tombasis

15

The village of Arachova, perched 3.000 feet above sea level on the side of Mount Parnassos, is famous for its heroism in the 1821 independence war, its red wine and hand woven goods.

*

A 980 mètres d'altitude, perchée sur les flangs du Parnasse, voilà Arachova, célèbre pour son héroïsme durant la revolution de 1821 et réputée pour son vin rouge et ses tapis de laine.

*

Fast 980 Meter hoch im Parnassgebirge liegt das malerische Dorf Arachova, das durch seine heldenhafte Haltung im griechischen Freiheitskrieg weithin bekannt wurde.

16

17

Upright and proud, the clock tower stands like a sentinel on a high rock. It was built in 1870 by the Abbot of Hosios Loukas. Opposite are the fir-covered slopes of Mt. Kirphis and below lies the ravine of the Pleistos...

*

La tour de l'horloge, construite en 1870 par le supérieur du monastère d'Hosios Loucas, se dresse fièrement au sommet d'un haut rocher. En face on aperçoit les versants du Kirphis recouverts de sapins et, en bas, le ravin du Pleistos...

*

Hoch oben auf einem Felsen steht der Glockenturm von Arachova. Gegenueber liegen die tannenbewachsenen Abhænge des Kirfis–Gebirges.

18

Phot. : A. Ververis

Phot. : S. Meletzis

Every year on April 23rd the people of Arachova celebrate the festival of St. George, their patron Saint. Young and old wear their fustanellas and dance to the sound of pipes.

*

Chaque année, le 23 avril, les habitants d' Arachova célèbrent la fête de Saint Georges. Jeunes et vieux portent la foustanelle et dansent aux sons du fifre et du tambour.

*

Alljaehrlich am 23 April feiern die Dorfbewohner das Fest des heiligen Georg des Schutzheiligen von Arachova.

Famed for their beauty, the women of Arachova are lovelier still in their national dress: the white woollen gown, the red apron, the silk blouse and the white ornamented headress, all woven and embroidered by hand...

*

Réputées pour leur beauté, les femmes d' Arachova, sont encore plus belles avec leur costume régional: La jupe de laine blanche, le tablier rouge, la blouse de soie et le fichu blanc qu'elles ont elles-mêmes tissés...

*

Die fuer ihre Schœnheit bekannten Frauen Arachovas sehen in ihrer Ortstracht noch reizvoller aus.

A last picture as we leave the village. A girl fetching water from the well. Her cheek is fresh with the snows of Parnassos and on her lips is the smile of early spring.

*

Une dernière image avant de quitter le village : Une jeune fille d'Arachova rentre de la souree où elle est allée chercher de l'eau. Ses joues ont la fraîcheur de la neige du Parnasse et sur ses lèvres fleurit le sourire du premier printemps.

*

Der Gang zum Brunnen, um das hier so kostbare Wasser zu holen, ist seit altersher eine Arbeit fuer die Frauen. Nicht immer freilich wird sie mit soviel Grazie verrichtet, wie auf unserem Bild.

25

Phot. : S. Meletzis

DELPHI ★ DELPHES

Phot. : S, Meletzis

A birds eye view of the sanctuary of Delphi. In the foreground the sacred way, the Treasury of the Athenians, the temple of Apollo and the theatre. Above the highway, the Museum. In the background the valley of the Pleistos, the plain of Amphissa and the sea.

Cette photo à vol d'oiseau nous présente l'enceinte sacrée de Delphes dans son admirable unité. On distingue la voie sacrée, le Trésor des Athéniens, le temple d'Apollon, le théâtre, au-dessus de la route le Musée et, au fond, la vallée du Pleistos, la plaine de Crissa et la mer.

*

Aus der Luft aufgenommen, zeigt der heilige Bezirk von Delphi seine ganze grossartige Einheit. Vorn die heilige Strasse mit dem Schatzhaus der Athener, dem Apollon-Tempel; rechts der Rundbau des Theaters. Im Mittelgrund, an der Autostrasse, liegt der moderne Bau des Museums.

Phot. : V. & N. Tombasis

Visitors coming by land are awestruck at the sight of the two beetling rocks of the Phaedriades, whose bulk rises bare and threatening above the valley.

*

Mais le visiteur arrivé par la route aperçoit d'abord les roches saisissantes des Phaedriades, qui nues et menaçantes, se dressent au-dessus de la vallée.

*

Der Besucher, der nicht den Seeweg gewæhlt hat, spuert hier mit leichtem Erschauern die Majestæt der steil aufragenden Phaedriaden-Felsen.

Below the highway to the left is the site called «Marmaria». Here are the sanctuary of Athena Pronaia, the Gymnasium and Palestra. Their supporting wall is preserved almost entire. Only the foundations, however, remain of the buildings where the athletes trained for the Pythian Games, and the round pool where they used to bathe.

*

A gauche de la route nous pouvons descendre vers Marmaria et visiter le temple d'Athéna Pronaia, le Gymnase et la Palestre.
Mais des bâtiments ou s'entraînaient les athlètes qui devaient se mesurer aux jeux Pythiques il ne subsiste plus que les fondations et le bassin rond où ils se baignaient.

*

Unterhalb der Strasse liegen der Tempel der Athena Pronaia und das Gymnasium. Von den Gebæuden, wo die Athleten ihre Uebungen machten, sind nur noch die Grundmauern erhalten.

Phot. : S. Meletzis   30

In the sanctuary of Athena Pronaia is the most graceful ancient building of Delphi, the Tholos. Three of its twenty doric pillars have been restored and a portion of the epistyle, with metopes and friezes representing combats of Amazons.

*

Quelques pas plus loin nous rencontrons le plus charmant des édifices antiques de Delphes, la Tholos avec trois de ses vingt colonnes doriques et un fragment de sa frise dont les métopes représentent un combat d'Amazones.

*

Wenige Schritte weiter sehen wir das zauberhafteste der delphischen Denkmæler, den Rundbau (Tholos) mit drei von zwanzig wiederaufgerichteten dorischen Sæulen und einem Teil des Architravs.

Phot. : V. & N. Tombasis

Phot. : P. Papachatzidakis

In striking contrast to the sanctuary of Athena Pronaia, the Castalian spring is dominated by the bulk of the Phaedriades rocks. The sacred spring flows between the sheer sides of the ravine.

*

En contraste absolu avec le temple d'Athéna Pronaia, le site de la fontaine Castalie est dominé par le masse des Phaedriades. C'est entre les flancs verticaux du ravin que coulent les eaux de la source sacrée.

*

Der Kastalische Quell mit seinen Nischen fuer Weihgeschenke befindet sich unter den Phaedriaden – Felsen.

Phot.: V. & N. Tombasis

On the sacred way we come suddenly to an elegant marble building. It is the restored Treasury of the Athenians, with its two doric pillars and thirty metopes, representing the labours of Hercules and Theseus. The originals are in the Museum. On the slmall triangular space in front stood the spoils of the battle of Marathon.

*

Tandis que nous gravissons la voie sacrée un élégant édifice de marbre apparait tout a coup devant nous. C'est le Trésor des Athéniens avec ses deux colonnes doriques et ses trente métopes qui représentent les travaux d'Hercule et de Thésée et dont les originaux se trouvent au Musée. Sur la petite place triangulaire qui s'étend devant le Trésor avait été déposé le butin de la bataille de Marathon.

*

Das Schatzhaus der Athener, das zu Beginn unseres Jahrhunderts wieder aufgebaut wurde. Seine Metopen zeigen die Arbeiten des Herkules und Theseus.

These fragments are all that is left of the famous temple of Pythian Apollo. A few half ruined pillars and the foundation stones. Phoebus has no longer a shelter or a prophetic laurel, but there is still the same wonderful view of the bare rocks, the mountain sides planted with olives and cypresses, the snakelike road down to the plain, sunlight playing on ancient rose-tinted stones and dancing among the leaves.

*

Voilà tout ce qui reste du fameux temple d'Apollon. Quelques colonnes a demi détruites et ses fondations. Phébus n'a plus de toit ni de laurier oraculaire, mais le site merveilleux demeure avec ses roches dénudées, ses vallées plantées d'oliviers et de cyprès, le ruban de la route qui serpente jusqu' à la plaine, le jeu du soleil dans les marbres antiques, dans le feuillage des arbres et les pierres rougeâtres, le brouillard qui descend du Parnasse et qui enveloppe tout dans ses voiles de buée.

*

Der Apollon–Tempel, in dem die Pythia weissagte. Der Anblick seiner Truemmer erinnert uns an ihre letzte Weissagung und ihre Klage ueber die Zerstœrung des Heiligtums.

Phot.: K. Dimitriades

Phot. : V. & N. Tombasis

Below the temple is a rough unhewn stone, the site of the sanctuary of the Earth, where the oracles were delivered before the building of the temple.

*

Au–dessous du temple une grosse pierre brute: C'est là que se trouvait le sanctuaire de Gaia et la pierre de la Sibylle, où l'on rendait l'oracle avant l'érection du temple.

*

Unterhalb des Tempel liegt ein unbehauener Stein: hier befand sich das Gaia-Heiligtum und der Stein der Sibylle, wo anfangs die Orakelsprueche gegeben wurden.

Opposite are the slender Ionic columns of the stoa of the Athenians and the skilfully fitted polygonal wall carved with names of freed slaves and victorious athletes.

*

En face les sveltes colonnes ioniques du portique des Athéniens et l'admirable mur polygonal. On peut y lire les noms d'esclaves affranchis, d'athlètes victorieux ainsi que des décisions prises par les Amphictyons.

*

Gegenueber stehen die ionischen Sæulen der Athener-Halle, dahinter die aus Kurven-polygonen kunstvoll zusammengefuegte Mauer. Sie berichtet uns von befreiten Sklaven, von Siegern im Wettkampf nnd von Beschluessen der Amphiktyonen.

43

Phot.: V. & N. Tombasis

Phot.: N. Emmanouil

44

Wandering in the sanctuary we see the relics of its former glory. Wild flowers grow amid the pillars and fallen stones. The olive is characteristic of the Delphic landscape.

*

De quelque côté que nous dirigions nos regards à l'intérieur de l'enceinte sacrée, nous ne verrons que les vestiges de son ancienne grandeur. Parmi les colonnes et les marbres brisés poussent les fleurs des champs. L'olivier vient compléter le paysage delphique.

*

Wohin wir auch blicken, sehen wir die Ueberreste der einstigen Majestæt. Heute bluehen zwischen und in den Steinen und Sæulen Feldblumen.

The ruins do not always date from classical times. The Romans added many buildings and works of art, such as this statue of a woman. Roman, too, are the stone steps.

*

Les ruines que l'on peut voir à Delphes ne datent pas seulement de l'antiquité classique. Les Romains y ont ajouté une foule d'édifices et d'ouvrages techniques. Cette statue de femme assise est romaine ainsi que l'escalier de pierre.

*

Hier ruhen nicht nur die Ruinen der klassischen Zeit. Auch die Rœmer bauten eine Anzahl Gebaeude und errichteten Kunstwerke. Die Frauenfigur im Vordergrund und die Treppe sind rœmisch.

45   Phot.: N. Emmanouil

Phot. : P. Papachatzidakis

Northwest of the temple is the finely proportioned theatre. The first «Delphic Festival» was held in 1927, inspired by Angelos Sikelianos and his wife, who produced the «Prometheus Bound» of Aeschylus.

*

Le théatre déploie sa courbe harmonieuse au nord-ouest du temple. C'est dans ce théatre que se déroulèrent, pour la première fois au printemps de 1927, les «Fêtes Delphiques», dont l'inspirateur était le poète Ange Sikelianos et l'animatrice sa femme Eva. C'est alors que fut représenté pour la première fois le «Prométhée enchainé» d'Eschyle.

*

In diesen antiken Theater fanden 1927 die Delphischen Festspiele statt, fuer die der Dichter Sikelianos und seine Frau Eva die Eingebung hatten. Man fuehrte den «Gefesselten Prometheus» des Aeschylos auf. Der Chortanz war nach antiken Vasenbildern inszeniert.

Phot. : P. Papachatzidakis

Phot. : V. & N. Tombasis

48

49

...hree years later, at the second Delphic Festival, the ...ment of the «Suppliant Women» was added to that ...f Prometheus. The ancient theatre is empty now. But ...e Delphic idea has taken root. Soon there will be a ...Delphic Centre» founded there, where men of culture ...om all over the world can meet, as in the days of the ...mphictyons.

*

...rois ans plus tard, aux gémissements de Prométhée ...nt venues s'ajouter les lamentations des «Suppliantes». ...ujourd'hui les gradins du théâtre antique sont vides. ...ais l'idée Delphique a pris racine et l'on va bientôt ...nder à Delphes le «Centre Delphique» qui réunira, comme ...s Amphictyonies, les intellectuels du monde entier.

*

...rei Jahre spæter kam die Auffuehrung von «Die Schutz-...ehenden». Der Chor wurde zum Vorbild fuer alle spæte-...n Inszenierungen. Heute sind die Sitzreihen des anti-...n Theaters leer. Die Delphische Idee aber hat Wurzel ...fasst und bald wird in Delphi das internationale «Del-...hische Zentrum» gegruendet.

Phot.: S. Meletzis

Phot.: V. & N. Tombasis

Phot. :´ S. Loul

Everywhere there are pill
torn from their base, brok
inscriptions and capita
fallen marbles–calling to mi
the verses of Paul Nirvana

«No longer has the God
home or prophetic laur
In the rocky waste the Pyth
rav
On the Phaedriades the lig
falls p
And Castalia weeps tea
silent tear

De tous côtés des colonnes
isolées, des fragments d'inscriptions, des chapiteaux et
des débris de marbre épars
nous rappellent que «Le dieu
n'a plus de toit ni de laurier
oraculaire...»

*

Ueberall Ruinen, die uns
an das letzte Orakel erinnern:
«Der Gott hat kein Obdach
mehr...».

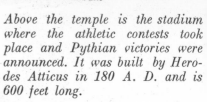

Phot.: V. & N. Tombasis

Above the temple is the stadium where the athletic contests took place and Pythian victories were announced. It was built by Herodes Atticus in 180 A. D. and is 600 feet long.

*

Le stade ou avaient lieu les jeux Pythiques. Il a etè construit par Herode Atticus et sa longueur est de 177,5 metres.

*

Das Stadion, wo Wettkæmpfe stattfanden und die Sieger der Pythischen Spiele bekanntgegeben wurden. Es wurde von Herodes Atticus gegen 180 A. D. gebant.

53

Phot. : S. Meletzis

5

55 Phot. : V. & N. Tombasis

... the 1927 Delphic Festival, con-
... similar to those of ancient
... took place in the stadium,
... the Pyrrhic war dance.

*

... des Fêtes Delphiques de 1927,
... jeux semblables a ceux de l'
... iquité se sont déroulés dans
... stade...

*

... den Delphischen Festspielen
... fuehrte man auch Kriegs-
... ze und Wettkæmpfe vor, wie
... vor ueber 2000 Jahren statt-
... unden hatten.

Phot. : S. Meletzis

57 *It is time to visit the Museum, and all the works of art found in Delphi.*

*

Mais il est temps de visiter le Musée où l'on peut admirer toutes les oeuvres d'art.

*

58 *Das Museum von Delphi.*

The archaic Sphinx of Naxos. * *Le Sphinx des Naxiens.* * *Die Sphinx der Naxier.*

The only sculptures saved from the Temple of Pythian Apollo are fragments from the pediments of the temple built by the Alcmeonides in 514 B.C. and destroyed in 372 B.C. Apollo, his mother Leto and sister Artemis were shown on the eastern pediment.

*

De toutes les sculptures du temple d'Apollon seuls subsistent les frontons du temple construit par les Alcméonides en 514 et détruit en 372. Apollon, sa mère Léto, sa soeur Artémis ornaient le fronton est et ont été trouvés au cours des fouilles.

*

Vom Apollo–Tempel ist nur ganz wenig gerettet worden. Hier einige Figuren–Fragmente des aelteren Tempels: Apollo, seine Mutter Leto, und seine Schwester Artemis.

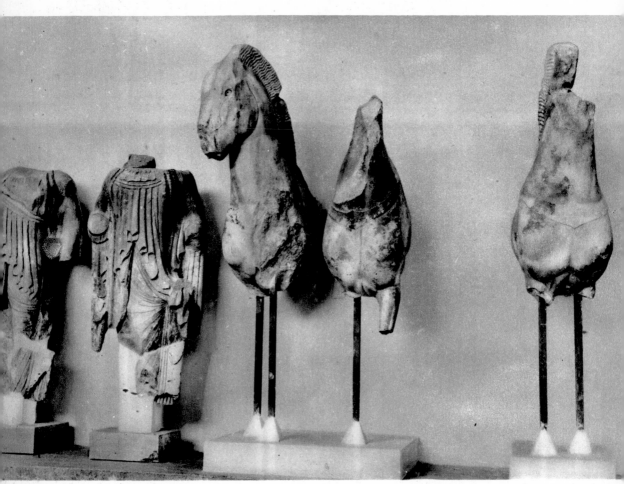

Phot.: V. & N. Tombasis

One of the Museum's most interesting exhibits, the «Omphalos». According to ancient tradition it represented the Navel of the Earth, believed to be situated at Delphi. The carvings on it are known as «Diadems», chains of wool plaited together to resemble a net.

*

Une des pièces les plus intéressantes du Musée, l'«Omphalos». D'après la tradition antique il figurait le nombril de la terre qui se trouvait à Delphes. Il est orné de «Stemmata», c'est a dire des cordons de laine tressés de façon a former une sorte de filet.

*

Der Omphalos von Delphi, den die Alten fuer den Nabel der Welt ansahen.

Phot.: V. & N. Tombasis

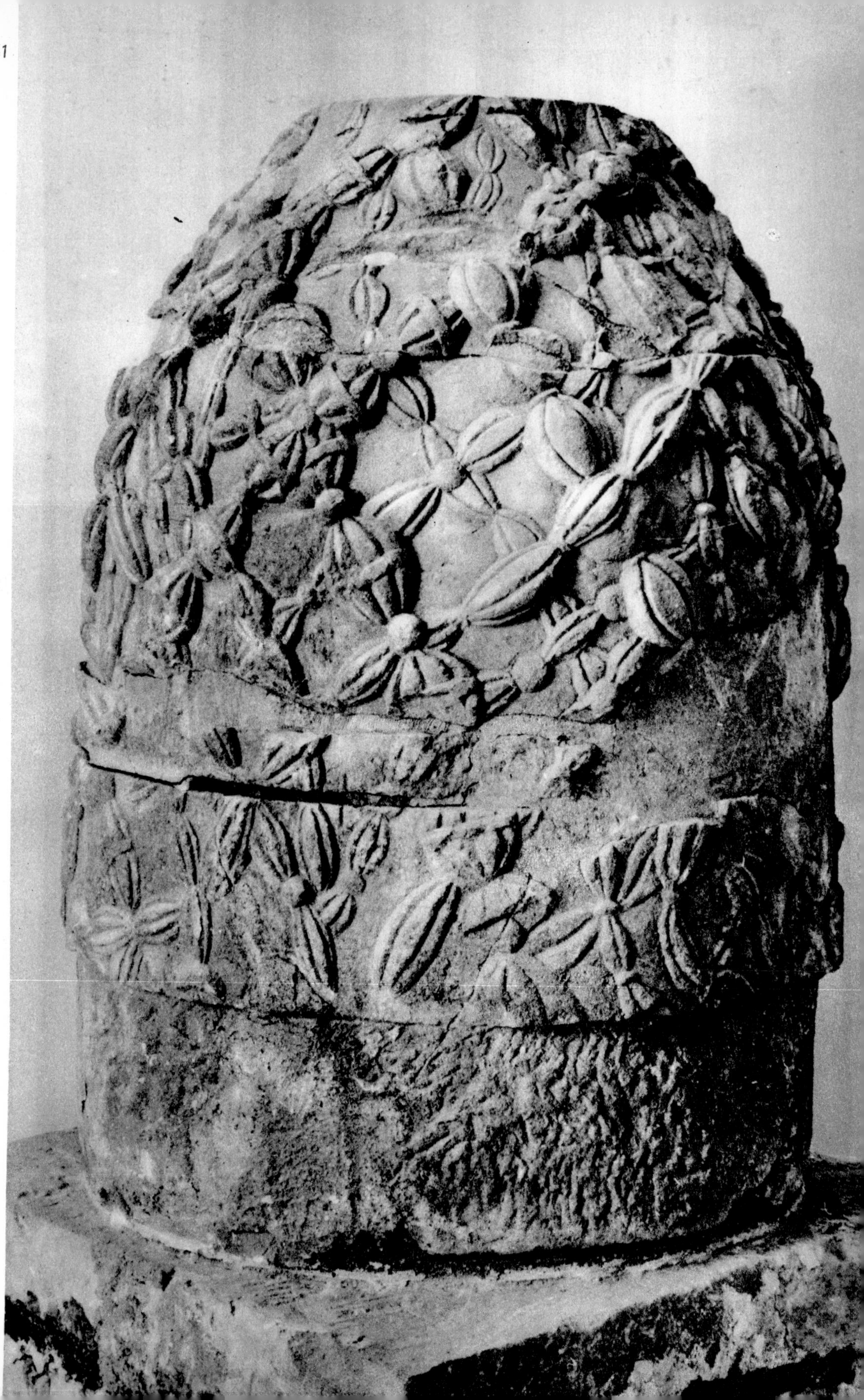

*One of the finest buildings in the sanctuary of Apollo was the treasury of the Siphnians.
*Un des plus beaux edifices de Delphes. Le trésor des Siphniens.
*Das Schatzhaus der Siphnier. Es wurde im Museum in Originalgrœsse wieder aufgebaut.

Phot. : V. & N. Tombasis

...is pediment represents Hercules' struggle
...r the Delphic Tripod. In the centre Athena
...empts to stop him, while Apollo tries to
...gain possession of the Tripod.

*

...fronton du trésor représente Héraclès
...tant d'enlever le trépied delphique. Au
...lieu Athéna tâche de l'en empêcher, tandis
...'Apollon veut reprendee son bien.

*

...ieser Fries stellt den Kampf um den del-
...ischen Dreifuss dar. Herakles wollte ihn
...hlen, aber Pallas Athena wehrt ihn ab.

...the model the pediment has been complet-
..., as have the archaïc Caryatids support-
...g the frieze and roof. The less damaged
...e, of the two originals, is charming.

*

...ur la reconstitution du trésor, le fronton a
...é complété ainsi que les Caryatides archaï-
...es. L'original, que l'on voit ici, nous
...arme toujours par sa grâce et sa douceur.

*

...uch die Karyatiden des Siphnier—Hauses
...nd ergaenzt; lediglich fuer eine war ein
...osses Fragment der echten vorhanden.

The most beautiful part of the treasury of the Siphnians is its wonderful frieze. The north side is the best preserved and shows the battle against the Giants. Gods, goddesses, demigods, on foot and in chariots, fight and defeat the iron-clad giants. Athena strikes a giant with her spear. Ares fights three at once, and Hermes is fighting two other giants. Hercules is helping the goddess Cybele, sitting in a chariot drawn by two lions. Further forward are Apollo and Artemis, fighting side by side.

*

Mais le chef–d'oeuvre du trésor des Siphniens est sa frise admirable. La partie nord, mieux conservée que les autres, représente la bataille des Géants. Dieux, déesses, demi-dieux, les uns à pied, les autres sur des chars, combattent contre les géants bardés de fer et remportent la victoire. Athéna frappe un géant de son javelot. Arès se bat contre trois tandis que, devant lui Hermès en affronte deux autres. Héraclès aide la déesse Cybèle, montée sur un char tiré par deux lions. Et enfin, unis dans le combat, Apollon et sa soeur Artémis.

*

Das am besten erhaltene Relief des Siphnier–Hauses stellt den Kampf mit den Gigan-ten dar, die schliesslich von Gœttern, Gœttinnen, Halbgœttern und anderen Helden besiegt werden.

65

* *This relief shows Athena descending fully armed from a chariot*
* *Ce relief représente la déesse Athéna descendant tout armée de son char ou sont attelés des chevaux ailés dont Hermès attrape tes rênes.*
* *Diese Skulptur zeigt die Gœttin Athena, wie sie aus ihrem Wagen steigt.*

* These horses, remind us of the wonderful horses of the Parthenon.

* Ces chevaux nous rappellent les admirables cavaliers du Parthénon.

* Die Skulpteure haben ihre ganze Kunstfertigkeit in die Ausbildung der Pferdekœrper gelegt. Man erinnert sich an die Parthenonpferde.

The lively scene on the eastern side is the fight over the body of Patroclus. Friends and enemies struggle over the dead hero as Homer describes:

«.....Warre here increast his heate.
The whole day long, continually the labour and the sweate.
The knees, calves, feete, hands, faces smear'd of men that Mars applied
About the good Achilles' friend....»

La scène figurant sur le côté est de la frise est le combat qui se déroule au-dessus du cadavre de Patrocle. Autour du mort se battent amis et ennemis, comme le décrit si bien Homère dans l'Iliade.

*

Die Ostseite zeigt den Kampf ueber dem Leichnam des Patroklos. Rund um den toten Helden kæmpfen Freund und Feind, wie Homer schreibt:

«Also tobten sie gleich dem Feuer; es hætte wohl niemand
Jetzt gewusst, ob Sonne und Mond noch stuenden am Himmel.
Denn es waren vom Nebel umhuellt die Helden, soweit sie
Standen im Kampf um die Leiche des edlen Menoitiossohnes.

The battle between Greeks and Trojans is watched on high by the gods of Olympus.
Zeus is seated on his throne, behind him Apollo with his head turned towards his mother
and sister, opposite them Athena with two other goddesses.

«...Then Jove charged Themis from Olympus' top
To call a court, she every way disperst, and summoned up all deities.
...All at his court that is king of gods
Assembl'd, and in lightsome seats of admirable frame
Performed for Jove by Vulcan sate.»

Du haut de l'Olympe les dieux assitent à ce combat entre Grecs et Troyens. Zeus est assis sur son trône. Derrière lui Apollon a la tête tournée vers sa mère et sa soeur. En face d'eux est assise Athéna avec deux autres déesses.

*

Den Kampf zwischen Troern und Griechen verfolgen die Gœtter vom Himmel aus; Zeus sitzt auf seinem Thron, hinter ihm Apollo, den Kopf zu Mutter und Schwester gewandt.

«Zeus nun gebot der Themis die Gœtter zum Rath zu berufen.
Von des Olympus Haupt des vielgebognen, und ringsum
Wandelte Jen' und gebot sich um Zeus Palast zu versammeln.
Als sie im Haus nur ankamen des Donnerers Zeus Kronion.
Rings in gehauenen Hallen nun sassen sie, welche dem Vater
Selbst Hephæstos gebaut mit erfindungsreichen Verstande...»

72

Metope from the Treasury of the Sikyonians. The Dioscuri, t h e Apharides and the stolen oxen.

*

Métope archaï-que du Trésor des Sicyoniens. On y voit les Dioscu-res et les Apha-rides avec les bœufs volés. .

*

Eine Metope vom Sikyonier Schatzhaus. Dioskuren und Aphariden mit den gestohlenen Ochsen.

Phot. : V. & N. Tombasis

An ancient me-tope from the treasury of the Athenians : Her-cules and the Ar-cadian stag.

*

Une des métopes du Trésor des A-théniens. Héra-clès et le cerf aux pieds d'airain.

*

Eine Reliefszene vom Schatzhaus der Athener : He-rakles mit dem Hirsch von Ke-rynia.

Phot. : V. & N. Tombasis

Two other me
topes from the
Treasury of the
A t h e n i a n s .
Theseus tames
the bull of Ma
rathon...

*

Deux autres mé
topes du trésor
des Athéniens.
Sur la première
Thésée terrasse
le taureau de
Marathon...

*

Noch zwei Me
topen vom Athe
ner Schatzhaus.
Theseus fæng
den Stier vor
Marathon...

...And defeats
the amazon An
tiope.

*

...Et sur la se
conde il est vi
ctorieux d'An
tiope, reine des
amazones.

*

Und hier be
siegt er die Ama
zone Antiope.

One of the most charming exhibits in the Museum is the group of the three acanthus dancers. Above their heads was a votive tripod.

*

Une des sculptures les plus attachantes du Musée, les trois danseuses de l'acanthe. Trois charmantes jeunes filles tenant d'une main leur courte tunique dansent légèrement sur les feuilles d'acanthe déroulées en volutes. Sur leurs têtes coiffées du «polos» à rayons était posé un trépied votif.

Phot.: V. & N. Tombasis

Die Akanthussæule mit den rei Tænzerinnen, die als Sockel eines Votivdreifusses diente. Man findet nicht eicht etwas Graziœseres in er antiken Skulpturkunst.

80

81

82

Phot.: V. & N. Tombasis

83

There are a multitude of other works of art
in the Museum of Delphi. The statue of a girl,
whose wonderful folds were copied from the
wet dress of the model; The lion-shaped gar-
goyles and the flower patterns of the Tholos;
An altar from the hellenistic era; The trunk
of an amazon.

*

Le Musée de Delphes offre à l'admiration du
visiteur une foule d'autres pièces d'art: une
statue aux plis admirables que l'artiste
parvenait a réussir en mouillant la robe
de son modèle, les chéneaux en tête de
lion de la Tholos, un autel de l'époque hellé-
nistique, une amazone dont seul le tronc
subsiste.

*

Ein Mædchenstandbild, bei dem es dem
Kuenstler gelang, den Faltenwurf des Kleides
vollendet wiederzugeben, aus hellenistischer Zeit.
Eine Amazone, von der nur der Kœrper ge-
borgen werden konnte.

84

Now we reach the last room in the Museum. In solitary state on his black marble pedestal is the most precious object in Delphi, the bronze Charioteer.

*

Nous arrivons maintenant à la dernière salle du Musée. Seul, debout sur son socle de marbre noir, nous attend le plus prestigieux chef-d'oeuvre de Delphes, l'aurige de bronze.

*

In der Mitte des letzten Saales ist auf einem schwarzen Marmorsockel der Wagenlenker aufgestellt. Er ist das wertvollste Stueck des Museums.

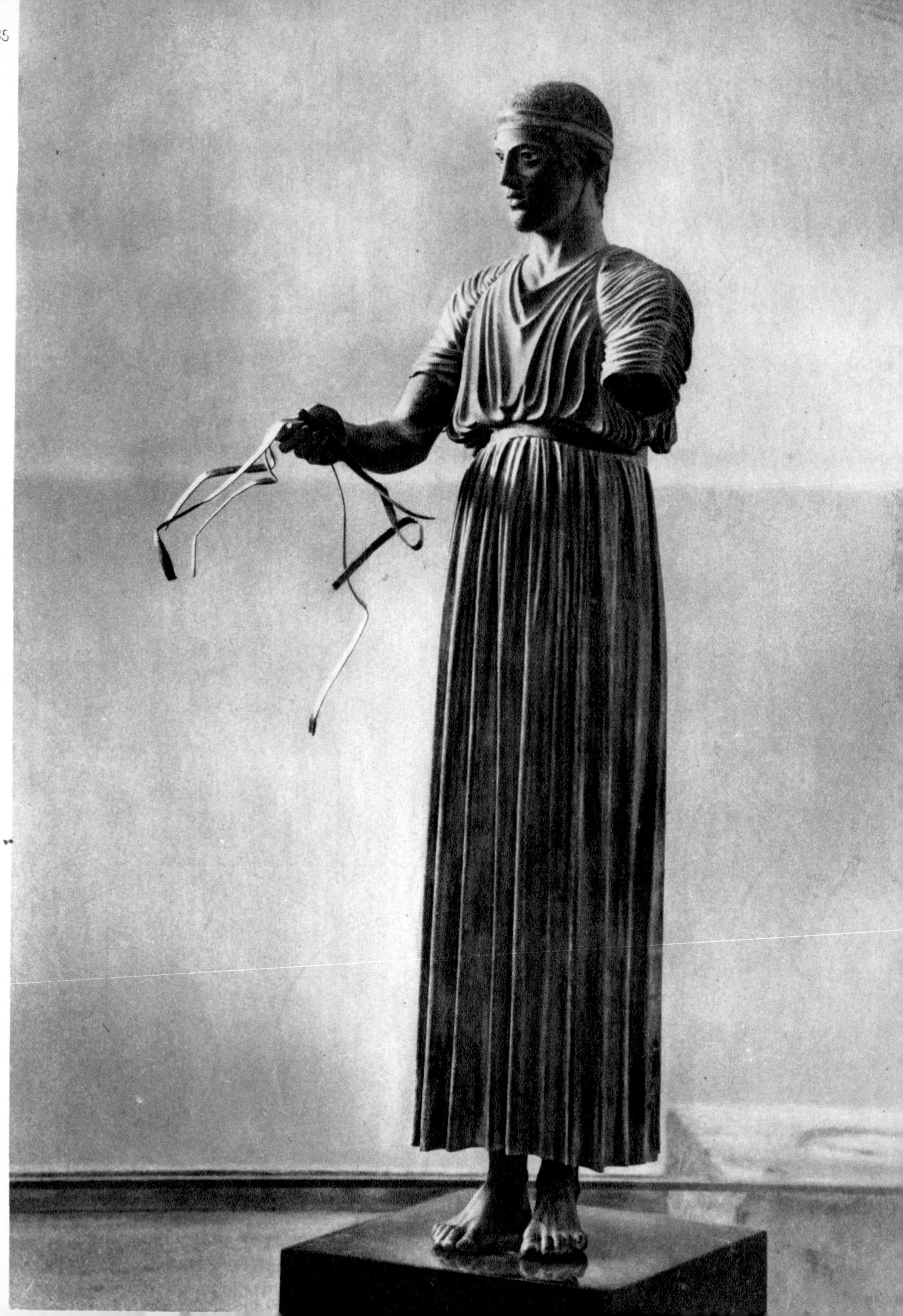

In his right, undamaged hand the Charioteer holds the reins of his chariot.

*

De sa main droite demeurée intacte l'aurige tient les rênes du char qu'il conduisait.

*

Mit der rechten Hand hælt der Wagenlenker die Zuegel des Streitwagens.

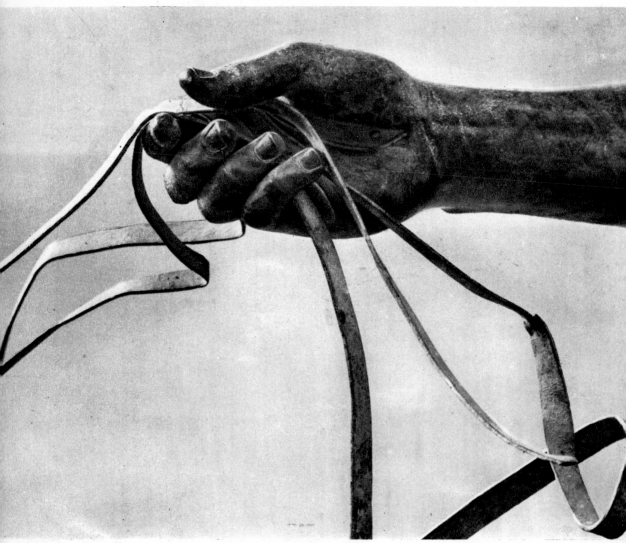

86

No other bronze statue has reached us in such good condition. The whites of his far-seeing eyes are made of enamel and the pupils are of onyx. They are shaded by fine metal eyelashes, so perfectly wrought that they seem to move. The mouth is half open as though about to speak. The more often we see the Charioteer, the more he keeps us spellbound.

*

→

Aucune statue de bronze ne nous est parvenue aussi bien conservée. Les yeux rêveurs fixés sur l'infini sont en émail blanc et en onyx. Les cils en métal sont si naturels que l'on croit les voir vibrer. Les lèvres entr'ouvertes semblent vouloir parler.

Die Kunst des Skulp-
teurs zeigt sich auch
gerade in den Einzel-
heiten. Keine andere
Kupferstatue blieb bis
in unsere Tage hinein
so gut erhalten wie
diese.

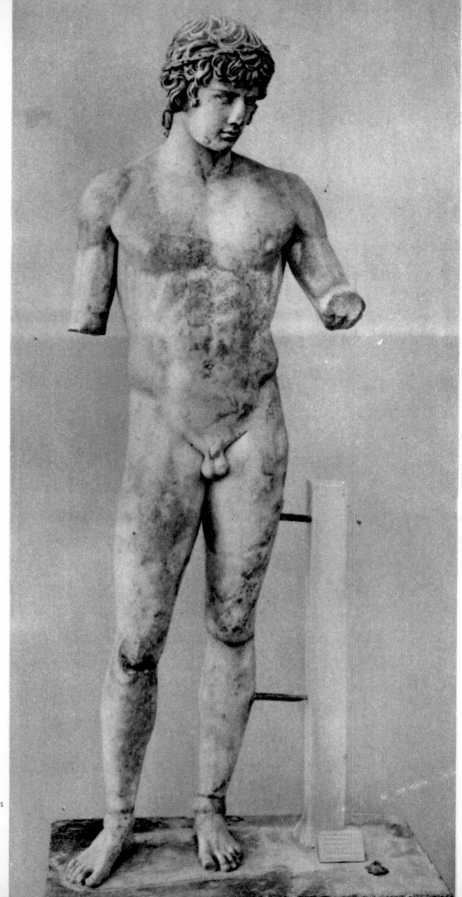

88

Phot. : P. Mylof

Much stronger and
more expressive is
this male head, the
work of an un-
known fourth cen-
tury artist.

*

Beaucoup plusforte
et plus expressive,
cette tête d'homme,
oeuvre d'un artiste
inconnu du IVe
siècle.

*

Ausdruck s v oll e r
und männlicher
ist dieser Kopf
eines unbekannten
Kuenstlers des vier-
ten Jahrhunderts.

Six centuries later in date than the bronze
Charioteer, the marble Antinoüs is a typical
example of art in the years of decadence. The
handsome head with its dark hair turns
mournfully aside. The eyes and mouth have
the bitterness of death.

*

De six siècles plus jeune que l'aurige de bronze
l'Antinoüs de marbre est une des oeuvres les
plus caractéristiques de l'époque de la déca-
dence. Sa belle tête aux cheveux bouclés est
penchée sur le côté, ses yeux et sa bouche
expriment l'amertume de la mort.

*

600 Jahre juenger ist dieser marmorne Anti-
noos, eines der besten Zeugnisse hellenistischer
Kunst. Mund und Augen sind schon um-
schattet von Todesbitternis...

Phot. : V. & N. Tombasis

The moment has come to rest. Any corner of the village has a unique view of the valley stretching to the sea.

Phot.: V. & N. Tombasis

91

92

Le moment est maintenant venu de prendre un peu de repos. N'importe quel endroit du village nous offre la vue magnifique de l'immense olivaie d'Amphissa qui s'étend vers la mer.

*

Ueber die Dæcher von Delphi hinweg geht der Blick hinunter in die Ebene von Amphissa mit ihren tausend und abertausend Olivenbæumen.

But it is better to enjoy the view from the new tourist hotel, with all the valley at its feet.

*

Mais il vaut anieux l' admirer de la terasse du nouvel hôtel qui a toute la vallée à ses pieds.

*

Aber man geniesst den sehoenen Anblick besser von der Terasse des neuen Touristen-Hotels.

93

Phot. : V. & N. Tombasis

94

Whether in spring, when the almond and cherry are in blossom, or in autumn Delphi has the same fascination. Three photographers, P. Mylov S. Meletzis and K. Dimitriades have captured spring in Delphi. V. Papaioannou prefers the autumn, when the mountains are clothed in airy veils of mist and the ancient stones become shining mirrors.

*

Que ce soit au printemps, lorque les amandiers et les cerisiers sont en fleurs, ou à l'automne avec les bourrasques et les averses, Delphes exerce un charme invincible mais particulièrement sur l'artiste. Trois photographes, P. Mylov, S. Meletzis et C. Dimitriadis ont vu chacun le printemps à Delphes sous un aspect différent. V. Papaïoannou, elle a davantage aimé l'automne.

*

Jede Jahreszeit hat in Delphi ihren besonderen Zauber. Vor dem majestætischen Hintergrund wird auch das selbstverstændlichste Naturereignis gleichsam zum dramatischen Geschehen.

Phot.: V. & N. Tombasis

In those autumn months, the clouds covering Parnassos give the Delphic landscape a different character – calm and remote.

*

Durant les mois d'automne les nuées qui recouvrent le Parnasse donnent un aspect tout à fait différent au paysage delphique qui semble abandonné et oublié du monde.

*

Im Fruehjahr bluehen die Mandel–und Kirschbæume... im Herbst ist die Natur im Aufruhr. Wolken ziehen ueber die heiligen Stætten...

Phot.: P. Mylof

As *winter sets in, the summits of Parnassos are covered with snow. The pines and cypresses take on a mournful note and the sky is overcast.*

*

Dès que l'hiver arrive les cimes du Parnasse se couvrent de neige, les pins et les cyprès s'assombrissent et le ciel s'alourdit.

*

...Bis sich im Winter die Parnassgipfel mit Schnee bedecken, Kiefern und Zedern sich dunkler färben und der Himmel schwer wird.

But in the highest part the new tourist hotel supplies comfort, warmth and good cheer...

*

Mais à l'endroit le plus haut de Delphes, le nouvel hôtel offre confort, chaleur et repos...

*

Am hœchsten Punkte aber befindet sich das neuerbaute Hotel. Da ist Waerme und Bequemlichkeit zu finden.

Phot. : V. & N. Tombasis

We pass the thousand-year old olive grove as we come down from Delphi. It spreads across the plain with over 500,000 trees. The famous Amphissa olives come from here.

Phot. : V. Papaioannou

Phot.: M. Chroussaki

Below the old castle lies the town of Amphissa, once known as Salona and famous in medieval days. Now it has the peaceful beauty of a provincial centre.

*

Sous son vieux château Amphissa, l'ancienne Salona, «Ville fameuse au temps des Grecs», a aujourd'hui le charme tranquille de la province grecque.

*

Unterhalb der alten Festung aus der Frankenzeit fuehrt Amphissa heute das friedliche Leben einer griechischen Provinzstadt.

Phot. : V. & N. Tombasis

The valley of the Mornos between Parnassos and Korakas is spanned by two bridges. Romantic travellers will enjoy the idyllic landscape from the stone arch of the medieval bridge. Those pressed for time will prefer the modern iron bridge.

*

Deux ponts joignent les rives de Mornos, entre le Parnasse et le Coracas. Les promeneurs romantiques passeront par le pont de pierre médiéval et s'arrêteront pour admirer la sérénité du site, mais les voyageurs pressés préfèreront le pont moderne.

*

Zwischen dem Parnassos und dem Korakas–Berg fuehren diese zwei Bruecken ueber eine Schlucht des Mornos–Flusses. Die eine neu erbaut, die andre aus der Byzantinischen Zeit.

The name of Naupaktos recalls former glories. Its eastle during four hundred years passed from the venetian to the Turkish rule.

*

Mais a Naupacte le souvenir de la gloire passée est toujours vivant: Son château, qui a connu tant de sièges quatre cents ans durant, passait des mains des Vénitiens à celles des Turcs.

*

In Naupaktos bleibt die Erinnerung an einstigen Ruhm lebendig. Die hohe Burg ging waehrend vierhundert Jahre von den Haenden der Venezianer in tuerkische Haende ueber.

Phot.: V. & N. Tombasis

Phot.: V. & N. Tombasis

Lepanto is the venetian name for Naupaktos and the famous battle of 1571 was fought off its shores. From this quiet little harbour the proud Turkish armada set sail...

*

Les Vénitiens appelaient Naupacte Lépanto et c'est sous ce nom qu'est connue la fameuse bataille navale du 7 Octobre 1571, qui a eu lieu non loin de son littoral. C'est de ce petit port tranquille qu'était partie l'armada turque jusqu' alors invincible...

*

Die Venezianer nannten Naupaktos Lepanto. Unter diesen Namen ist die beruehmte Seeschlacht des 7 Oktobers 1571 bekannt.

...To return defeated after heavy losses, with strength and reputation gone.

*

...Pour y revenir vainque et décimée, ayant perdu pour toujours sa force et sa renommée.

*

Von diesen kleinen Hafen war die bis dahin «unbesiegbare» tuerkische Armada ausgebrochen, um besiegt und dezimiert zurueckzukehren.

Phot. : V. & N. Tombasis

We are near the end of our journey, in Antirrion. Like an outstretched hand, the twin fortress of Rion beckons from the opposite side. The crossing is over in less than half an hour and we set foot in the Peloponnese, where new beauties and experiences await us. We follow their call!

*

Nous voici maintenant arrivés a la fin de notre voyage à Antirrion. De l'autre côté du golfe apparait le château de Rion. En moins d'unedemi-heure nous arrivons au Péloponnèse. De nouvelles merveilles nous y attendent...

*

Nun sind wir am Ende unserer Reise. In Antirrion erwartet uns die Fæhre, um uns ueber den korinthischen Golf hinueber nach Rion auf der Peloponneshalbinsel zu bringen. Dort erwarten uns neue Schœnheiten. Gehen wir und freuen wir uns ihrer!

Phot. :

V. & N. Tombasis

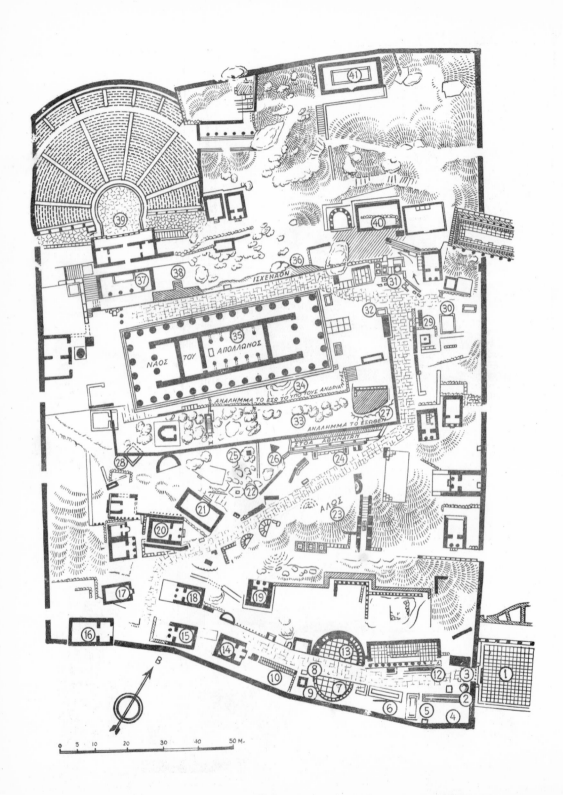

ΙΣΧΕΝΔΩΝ

ΝΑΟΣ ΤΟΥ ΑΠΟΛΛΩΝΟΣ

ΑΝΑΛΗΜΜΑ ΤΟ ΕΣΩ ΤΟ ΥΠΟ ΤΟΥΣ ΑΝΔΡΙΑ

ΑΝΑΛΗΜΜΑ ΤΟ ΕΞΩΘΕΝ

ΣΤΟΑ ΑΘΗΝΑΙΩΝ

ΑΛΩΣ

Β

0 5 10   20   30   40   50 Μ.

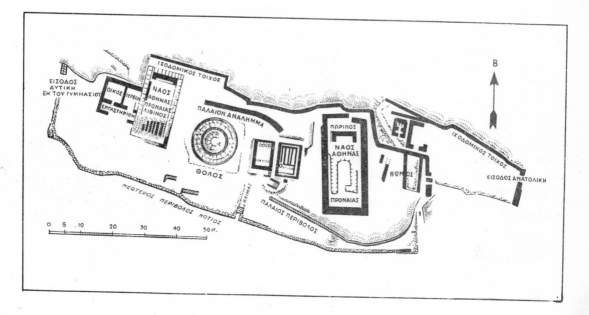

← SANCTUARY OF DELPHI

1. Roman Agora. **2.** Phayllos Trench. **3.** Ex-voto of the Corcyrans. **4.** Ex-voto of Marathon. **5.** Troian war memorial. **6.** Seven against Thebes. **7.** The descendants (Argive-ex voto). **8.** Ex-voto of the Riginians. **9.** Statue of Hieron **10.** Ex-voto of the Tarantines. **11.** The Spartan admirals. **12.** Ex-voto of the Arcadians. **13.** The Argive kings. **14.** Treasury of the Sikyonians. **15.** Treasury of the Siphnians. **16.** Treasury ef the Thebans. **17.** Treasury of the Boeotians. **18.** Treasury of the Syracusans. **19.** Treasury of the Knidians. **20.** Treasury of the Athenians. **21.** Senate house. **22.** Sanctuary of Earth-Rock of Sibyl. **23.** Alôs **24.** Stoa of the Athenians. **25.** Sphinx of the Naxians. **26.** Victory of Paionius. **27.** Polygonal wall. **28.** Polygonal wall. **29.** Tripod of Plataea. **30.** Chariot of the Rhodians. **31.** Acanthus. **32.** Altar of the Chians. **33.** Lower terrace. **34.** Terrace of supporting walls. **35.** Temple of Apollo. **36.** Ischegaon. **37.** Chase of Alexander. **38.** The Charioteer. **39.** Theatre. **40.** Ex-voto of Daochos. **41.** Clubhouse of the Knidians.

LE SANCTUAIRE DE DELPHES

1. Agora Romaine. **2.** Base de Fayllos. **3.** Taureau des Corcyréens. **4.** Base de Marathon. **5.** Le «cheval Dourien». **6.** Les Sent de Thebes. **7.** Les Epigones. **8.** Offrande des Righiens. **9.** Statue de Hieron. **10.** Offrande des Tarentins. **11.** Amiraux des Lacédémoniens (Aigos Potamos). **12.** Offrande des Arcadiens. **13.** Les rois d' Argos. **14.** Trésor des Sicyoniens. **15.** Trésor des Siphniens. **16.** Trésor des Thébains. **17.** Trésor des Béotiens. **18.** Trésor des Syracuse **19.** Trésor des Cnidiens. **20.** Trésor des Athéniens. **21.** Bouleuterion. **22.** Sanctre de la Terre-Rocher de la Sibylle. **23.** Alôs. **24.** Portioqe des Athéniens. **25.** Sphinx des Naxiens. **26.** Victoire de Péonios **27-28.** Mur polygonal. **29.** Trépied de Platées. **30.** Char des Rhodiens. **31.** Acanthe. **32.** Autel d' Apollon (offrande de Chios). **33-34.** Terasse du soubassement. **35.** Temple d' Apollon. **36.** Ischegaon **37.** Chasse d' Alexandre. **38.** Aurige. **39.** Thétre. **40.** Offrande du Thessalien Daochos. **41.** Lesché des Cnidiens.

DAS HEILIGTUM VON DELPHI

1. Roemische Agora. **2.** Phayllos-Saeule. **3.** Weihgeschenk von Kerkyra. **4.** Weihgeschenk von Marathon. **5.** Das «Trojanische Pferd». **6.** Die «Sieben gegen Theben». **7.** Die Epigonen (Argiver—Weihgeschenk). **8.** Weihgeschenk der Riginier. **9.** Statue des Hiero. **10.** Weihgeschenk der Tarentiner. **11.** Die Admirale von Sparta. **12.** Weihgeschenk der Arkadier. **13.** Die Koenige von Argos. **14.** Schatzhaus der Sikyonier. **15.** Schatzhaus der Siphnier. **16.** Schatzhaus der Thebaner. **17.** Schatzhaus der Boetier. **18.** Schatzhaus von Syrakus. **19** Schatzhaus von Knidos. **20.** Schatzhaus der Athener. **21.** Versammlungshaus. **22.** Heiligtum der Sibylle. **23.** Alôs. **24.** Halle der Athener. **25** Sphinx der Naxier. **26.** Siegessaeule des Paionios. **27-28.** Polygonalmauer. **29.** Dreifuss von Plataeae. **30.** Wagen der Rhodier. **31.** Akanthus. **32.** Altar von Chios. **33-34.** Untere Terrasse. **35.** Apollon-Tempel. **36.** Ischegaon. **37.** Alexanderjagd. **38.** Der Wagenlenker. **39.** Theater. **40.** Daochos Weihgeschenk. **41.** Lesche von Knidos.

THIS BOOK IS ONE OF THE FIRST ISSUED IN THE TOURISTIC SERIES «THE FACE OF GREECE». PRINTED BY THE NEW ROTOGRAVURE PROCESS, BY M. PECHLIVANIDIS & Co. ARTISTIC SUPERVISION : KOSTAS DIMITRIADIS

★ ★

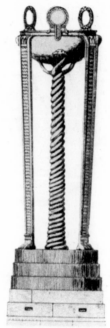

CE LIVRE DE LA PREMIÈRE SÉRIE DES PUBLICATIONS TOURISTIQUES »VISITONS LA GRÈCE». EST SORTI DES PRESSES - HELIOGRAVURE M. PECHLIVANIDIS ET Cie. DIRECTION ARTISTIQUE: C. DIMITRIADIS

DIESES BUCH DER ERSTEN REIHE DER VERÖFFENTLI-CHUNGEN FÜR DEN FREM-DENVERKEHR «LERNT GRIE-CHENLAND KENNEN». WURDE IM TIEFDRUCKVERFAHREN BEI DER FA. M. PECHLIVANI-DIS & Co GEDRUCKT . KÜNSTLERISCHE LEITUNG VON KOSTAS DIMITRIADIS

The first issue consists of the following publications:

★

Cette première série comprendra les publications suivantes:

★

Die erste Reihe umfasst folgende Veroeffentlichungen:

TINOS (Island of Miracles), • ARGOLIS (Mycenae – Tiryns – Nafplion – Epidaurus) • ANCIENT ATHENS • BYZANTINE ATHENS • ATHENS TODAY • DELPHI • OLYMPIA • MOUNT ATHOS • SARONIC ISLANDS (Aegina – Poros – Hydra – Spetsae) • THE CYCLADES • MYKONOS – DELOS • CRETE • SALONICA • RHODES • CORFU (Kerkyra) • MISTRA — SPARTA • YANNINA • THE ACROPOLIS OF ATHENS

A second issue will follow

★

Une deuxième série, conplétera le corpus de ces publications

★

Eine zweite Reihe wird folgen

PUBLISHERS M. PECHLIVANIDIS & Co

PRINCIPAL DISTRIBUTORS: "ATLANTIS,, S.A. KORAI 8 - ATHENS